The Dedication

I dedicate this book to all those who had their hearts broken.
To the ones who never gave up on love. It's hard to love, especially with all that has happened in life. It is better to love with passion and to overcome obstacles than to be bitter and lonely. I hope these poems bring you pleasure and romance. Thank you.

When Darkness Loves

Dark Romance, Volume 1

Michael Dimenco and Wolffe

Published by Reaperblack6, 2023.

WHEN DARKNESS LOVES

First edition. August 31, 2023.

Copyright © 2023 Michael Dimenco and Wolffe.

ISBN: 979-8223960881

Written by Michael Dimenco and Wolffe.

Table of Contents

My Raven

Coal-colored morning,
stars going to bed.
Winds calling from the west,
a whisper to my heart.
My raven is so close,
almost as close as my skin.
Millions of people cry,
and millions of demons lie.
Thunderstorms come and go,
just as waves flow to and fro.
Under a blue sunset,
she stands by the shoreline.
Love whispers into her heart,
she waits by the rocks.
My raven glows like stars,
precious gems now before her.
Dark cries from a grave,
a frightened sound.
My heart conceivably,
locked in the shadow.
Hiding behind pain,
yet she waits like a rose in the rain.
To free me from a tedious past.

Halo on Fire

Rigid mountains break
sheer desire beyond transmission.
Turned into a fiery rain,
alone with my ghoulish pain.
The world is so dead and fake,
yet even this thunderous pity.
I see a halo on fire.
Never did true passion hit,
Not until my heart was stolen.
As a ship sails,
my hunger grows bolder.
Within a second,
blood drips from my chest.
Ashy dreams come like ghosts,
vivid love just beyond my cynical lips.
Scratching in a ceramic coffin,
laid to unrest with yellow roses.
Yet I can taste the halo on fire,
only in my restless skin tomb.
Collect a hundred kisses in black,
stones lie as others do.
Let a feisty frosty winter blow,
a smoke burning in a tired hand.
Yet silence became an enemy,
She knows the power of desire.
Drip, drip onto my iron.
A teasing blow to capture my woe.

A halo on fire just below my sight.
Another night of fantasy and pleasure,
I will never know.

Fear Romance

Dark sun rising,
a crimson smile on her face.
Eroding defenses with touches,
awkward moment dancing.
Timeless melodies float in the cool air,
she swirled around like a tornado.
The deep passion burns like a candle.
Drowning in a sea of fear.
A dream came as stars slept,
nightmare death scape calling.
Skeletons parade before my vault,
Shackled to a sick regret.
Restore my soul with kisses,
pounce on the flames of fear.
Verify my dying existence.
Her love is dangerous,
her lust consumed souls.
Yet, I live in fear.
Is it because of her? No!
Broken hearts bleed like a volcano.
Forever to mend,
but to miss her kiss is like
forgetting to breathe.
As I fear romance,
she fears loneliness.
At times, my words fail.
My wings cover her from

an icy world.
Committed to love,
dressed her in a golden veil.
To love her beyond forever
is my scared duty.

Seven Gems (Death Kite Mix)

Locked in hell,
seven gems awakened.
Not the flames of death,
but of love that unites souls.
Time is a wicked wine,
that lies with a smooth taste.
Nightmares and lost heart,
Disdained by foolish ghouls.
Trapped by a thin wire,
yet entertained by tulips.
Red tulips and dead ones too,
watching them return again and again.
Scorching my soul with words,
dressed in seven gems dipped in death.
Lost in her eyes,
an amber hue that is a torturous pleasure.
Down into the caller of desire,
cuffed to a block of dreams.
Her love is stronger than drugs.
Cast into the cold waters,
upwards into a new sky.
By an hours' fading edge,
worlds ablaze from love.
Cornerstone in Destiny,
Tasting blood by night.
Tossed into a mausoleum,
Haunted by her desire.

I'm hers until the last days
of the universe.

Seven Gems

Only on a spring day,
a blue crow will fly.
Just like love,
can't be caught but longed for.
Beaches wrapped full of people,
dangerous of romance
stalk-like sharks.
Evening tide by a greenish tide,
lost in mechanical thoughts.
Waiting for a colorful sunset,
dressed by sand.
Like a raven is silent,
my heart is quiet.
three hundred women walk by,
sadness fills my hand.
Not an angel among them,
not a single gem.
Lucky me for now,
refreshed by a playful tide.
Gentle laughter from the sea,
breathtaking sights,
seven gems in the sky.
Reflecting in jealous waters,
a smile like no other.
By the sound of waves and birds,
a kind cup of coffee is my friend.
Stars start to undress before my eyes,

and hot food tickles my nose.
Yet I wait by this sandy shore,
Wails of joy somewhere out
past the stones.
Somewhere beyond my vision,
a watery angel calls.
By the edge of life and death,
a reeking of blood and bone.
A tale of sailors comes to mind,
struck an eerie violin chord.
Sensing danger of high order,
a lullaby too hard to ignore.
Blasting horn of an ancient ship,
freed from a tempting lore.
Yet a rose washes up,
not blue, white or red but black.

Blue Diamond

The twinkle in the frigid night,
Rigid stones walk in the river.
Silent is the wind,
beautiful are the words she said.
Alone under a silver moon,
thinking of her as my heart cries.
A blue diamond among coal.
Stand with me by these hills,
let the crimson sun rays warm her.
Memories of her smiling overfilling me,
purple lips shatter my stony wall.
Brown eyes can make a priest weep,
trace my soul with her finger.
Washed in pure desire,
saddled with joy.
Ravens fly by without remorse,
by her side by heart flies freely.
Like a fresh cup of coffee,
a dream being resurrected from death.
Laying in her arms I can be an angel again.
Roaming in bed,
no longer dead.
Her compassion is beyond truth,
Hands playing with my hair.
Like a taco,
wrapped up in a city of doom sauce.
Afternoon arrives with a smile.

Watching my blue diamond
play in the symphonic sky.

On Fire

Gone are firefly's,
passion as deep as a emerald mine.
Her smile is as beautiful as a
baby mountain.
Dark skin radiance
makes music jealous.
Set the world on fire,
let our petals grow.
Autumn clashes with our desire,
Drown our sorrows in a bleak rainstorm.
Sitting by a copper fireplace,
Lips on lips and pain vanish like the wind.
Words play in our souls,
mischievous violinists taunt us playfully.
On fire for her,
on fire for me.
Sunlight falls gently around us,
covered in violets and crimson carnations.
Will the day play with us?
demons erode in fear.
Chained by life,
bound to suffer in death.
What remains is a dying storm?
In an eternity of fallen gods,
a war of love remains in our spirits.
love is from heaven,
while other junk can burn.

My eyes watch a dying sunset,
She snuggles in my arms.
An angel hidden by evil eyes,
safeguarded against humanity.
Forever I will remain her guardian and
remain on fire for her.

Silent Rose

Like rain to a field,
she needs love like no other.
A silent rose among a garden of thorns.
Emerald trees waste their melodies,
and streets of greed and lies are a plague.
Somewhere a rainbow dies,
She writes sadly in a journal.
Silent rose by a fragile window,
depressed by a dark time.
Ancient stains in a frigid room,
accompanied by her romance self-help books.
Her novels are dusty and
worn out like a WW2 soldier.
Silent colors can no longer scream,
Her hands were grey and dead.
Empty wishes collect in a brown jar,
and echoes of a world no longer disturb her.
Mind no longer strong but fearful,
empty bed without a lover for a thousand eons.
Trapped by self-pity and hate,
a crow cries by a sleepy fence.
A weak word fails to chase it off,
Born out of ashes.
Romance knows her heart,
denied a hundred suitors.
Broken engagements line her wall,
Rusty rings of gold and silver.

Matching her hair of age,
Silent Rose never calls to the one,
who wants him to call upon her.
I won't break the silence,
coffee cold in my hands.
Night breathes in resignation,
alone on the 7th floor.
evening is warm like chicken dinner.
Silent Rose remains hidden in a rusty cage,
Never bold to speak my name.
Too dependent on old ways,
now she can rust in her grave.
Pass away like a flame on a match.
Disgraced by her pride of yesterday.
Goodbye silent rose,
a waste of time and space.

Lost Lips

The color of Heaven
is the color of blood.
Not blue or red,
but as dark as evil.
Her lips are a trap,
followed by death.
Is it better to have lost lips?
The color of Hell
is the color of life.
Not yellow or blue,
but as weak as white.
Her body was a temple
but is a brothel now.
Her eyes burn with lust
as her lips lie and lie.
Is it better to have lost lips?
The color of Love
is the color of death.
Not black or purple,
but of crimson wine.
Now she grows old and alone,
while I remain a ghost of her life.
Is it better to have lost lips?

Buss of Violet Days

Frigid love cast into death's furnace,
collect the ashes from the flames.
Lost in a sea of destruction,
violet dreams flow as a river in me.
waiting by the nightmares within life,
her face is a blur within my heart.
Take my hand from the grave,
Kiss my aching lips one last time.
Inside my mind,
a hell exists that knows no mercy.
Love is a foreign entity,
even the River of Sorrow has control.
Can the stars weep like chocolate demons?
Violet eyes burn through this dire fog,
taking hold of the stone heart.
Breakthrough like a dark miner,
explore my body without hesitation.
Feed the darkness within her.
candles burn time,
Hot wax turns me into a mess.
Her kisses are that of a dragon's touch,
rough and unexpected.
On a breeze, we fly above all.
beyond a red sea lies paradise,
longing to taste me.
Her desire shatters my chains of sorrow.
Until the soft glow of morning comes,

we partake in a Devil's pleasure.

Glow of Twilight

Under a silver gloss of stars,
naked by her side.
Her face was gentle from the passion,
breathing like a beautiful storm.
Darkness stands afar,
cool air stirs like strings on a violin.
Only her smile could be seen,
rough life on the run.
Freedom is in my arms.
A rose knows no color
until it blooms by spring's rain.
Love is blind like a fallen demon.
Her eyes knew pain beyond this time,
frozen by sorrow for a month.
When the glow from a courageous sun,
defeats the winter within her.
Unlocking a lost soul,
fumes of a dead past haunt.
No longer consumed by evil,
scars visible to me alone.
Waiting by the sea of lust,
alone by a glacial ghost.
Taunting her through whispers,
ignoring empty words by a golden song.
Warming her with love,
Kissing her heart.
Loving until I bleed,

she takes my heart with ease.
Let the winter dance with death,
all of the sorrows can drown.
Eternity is her ring now.

LUST (Love Undergoes Supreme Torment)

Taste my desire,
drink of my death.
Drown in my passion,
let your dreams be mine.
Bow to the rose queen,
take a cold breath.
Run through a forest of darkness, opt t
Lay on my soul your heaviest regrets.
Down into the hull of night,
love is sweet as wine.
Naked bodies sweat
and groans escape into the darkness.
Gentle bites entice beautiful decay.
Tossed a boat in a thousand-foot sea,
She mounts me in playful rage.
A mad rhythm,
Fake anguish as she feigns death.
South winds weep,
and mountains sigh now.
Cuddled by a water flame,
night as hot as hell's furnace.
Touched by a wing,
dressed in a red-gold melody.
Early light starts to glow,
off to another shore.

Blue Moon

Sand burns souls,
her words slice my heart.
A butcher to release pain,
turned insane by daylight.
Bound by a blood oath,
lingering stains on my soul.
Come and drain me,
under a Blue Moon she glows.
Hunter was by nature,
an untamed wolf waiting to feast.
Green trees turn brown and black,
her love destroys darkness with ease.
Broken spoons cannot serve,
and neither can feeble people.
Come to me, baby,
drain my blood on the Blue Moon.
Let your snowy lips taste my blood,
silent are the graves by a jealous sea.
Time is meaningless,
the stars above will fall before her.
A queen above all others,
taunted by visions of sex.
Ever nippy from sober days,
lost in her eyes forever.

My Lie (Dreams in Blood mix)

Touched by fire tonight the wind calls,
alone on a skyscraper.
Shiny lives are snuffed out by knives,
yet even in grief there is freedom.
Down in a car's glare, there is romance.
Stand by the moon and watch me fall.
Inside a frigid madness,
a broken soul fights onward.
A wicked day in June brought
salvation to a crumbling mind.
Dark sunlight cannot glow,
her Light burned through my fog.
Never backing down,
Even as my demons scream in rage.
Her eyes chill my pain,
Her hands drown my sins.
Touched by fire and turned into gold,
No misery, only pleasure of time and light.
Loved by secret hours,
tormented by days in hell.
Freed by her hands now,
by a candle's edge we are one.

A Thousand Black Stars

So are the days numbered,
like a thousand black stars?
One can dream or one can die.
Nothing is promised,
not even love.
A sweet taste of darkness,
to hungry lips.
Let the dead crave meat,
a thousand black stars meet.
Take a look into a cracked mirror,
and face the bitterness of hopelessness.
Kiss the lips of a leper,
then freedom is like a fresh breeze
on a hot day.
Open the handles of torture,
a bleak stare into oblivion.
Torn heart,
Burning blood in a thousand milliseconds,
torched by freezing fire.
A dark passion covers me,
A whisper in an ear.
Turn towards me,
ghost of love.
Long dead but yearns for more,
A thousand black stars can weep now.
Only you can burn my darkness,
and set me free from this abuse.

The evil in my life,
be my knife against injustice.
Like a rose under glass,
I'm drowning in my pain.
Only you are beautiful enough
to scorch my demons.
Like a forgotten soldier,
my heart only knows seclusion.
Taste my lips for they are bitter,
just like rejection.
Love is unknown to my hands,
only the blood of my sins is known.
Only you are brave enough
to risk it all in my sea of troubles.
Lift a veil of redemption,
sing a song of light.
Kill these evil ghouls that
feast on my flesh.
Be confident and wise now,
let your warmth come and take
my coldness away.
Only you can free me,
Only you can take me away.
Dressed in radiant life,
Your heart is my lighthouse.
I want to be free from my cage,
Yearning to shatter this rotting iron
cage.
Only then I can be truly yours.

Take My Heart

Take me as I lay in fire,
Love me like the angel you are,
She is my wound of sorrow.
Beautiful Emerald eyes,
soft white skin.
Take my heart with you,
Let my heart moan for you,
Come and taste my humility.
Let the sun play for us,
by a whisper she haunts me.
Trapped by the desire of a killing lust,
Take me,
take me,
Never let go of my soul.
Reaching out from this frosty prison,
even in the shades of black.
Her love will save me,
Naked breast on my stomach.
Her kisses are as sweet
as Death's embrace.
Heaven may cry blood,
hell can freeze over before
we will ever end our love.

Red Dreams & Sexy Nights

Dirty Little girl sexy as a fallen angel
with red wings.
Eyes of blue-green,
like that of a sad ocean.
Dirty secrets that no one knows,
blazing the sulking sky with passion.
A dirty little girl loves like a goddess,
even demons run from her.
Undiluted light overflowing unto
this world.
Down into a mire of darkness and evil,
a sunken ship finds peace.
Romantic busses on my chest,
Igniting a deep passion within me.
Scorned by a dark terror,
evil bleeds on a table.
She brings a copper dream,
lashing out against Abaddon.
Fire can burn and the water cools
her love is unquenchable.
Silent are the days,
nights become wild.
Naked angel dreams,
stone weeps from ardor.
A dirty little girl holds me close,
soothing the searing sorrows within.
Her smile opens new desire in my soul,

lifting an empty heart to the stars.
Never bowing to enemies of love,
standing talk by heavens gate.

Black lipstick

Dark as night,
Lips of passion.
Face radiates like an
Angel.
Shallow breath at midnight's hour,
Blooming blood roses coming forth.
Black lipstick piercing
My anguished soul.
Lost in a tormented sea of emotions,
Glittering tears on my bronzed skin.
Icy words whispered into
my heart.
Black lipstick says passion in a deep dark level.
Hot night by a simmering river,
pounded by lust and bloody desire.
Ghosts scream in ecstasy,
Darkness surrounds us like a favorite blanket.
Dawn burns into the sky as a dragons
flame in forgotten mountains.
Torched by her touch,
A sweet breeze warms our paled bodies.
Swept away by petals of love,
We rest in our graves for another night.

5 Degrees of Pain

Love is sacrifice,
a faceless fate.
Yet a silver clock chimes,
a scared heart is soft-spoken.
Love cuts like a surgical knife,
removing the cancerous aspects.
Bleeding out the infection is loneliness,
yet the wounds are covered by
cheap bandages.
They are memories of past
destruction.
Burnt into the heart,
contradiction is bad medicine.
Yearning for love but not letting go,
Forcing the sickness unto another.
Burn them by sheer memory power,
Before me, I will strike you first.
Horrid value for them to digest.
Yet, nothing changes.
The mind remains in hell.
So much for love,
true joy tossed into the trash compactor.
Lying to oneself again.
Expecting the same outcome,
just add pain.
Won't change to be more suitable,
shallow pride haunts them like a ghoul.

Old age comes like a storm,
Only regrets and lies now.
Into the grave forever.

Loved in Autumn

Eyes of brown sorrow,
tourniquet for the dead.
Her smile called at 6 pm,
lost on a November evening.
A lonely cup of coffee,
Steam flowing like blood.
Stand by the black oak door,
waiting by the wet door.
Loved in autumn and drowned in winter,
never will the moon smile again.
touched by her flame,
Consumed by her desire.
rain is my pain as the night weeps,
her words were like diamonds; fake.
Autumn blows onward in silence,
Torching the bed with lies and lust.
Dreams come and go,
and scars are forever.
Soft nails against my skin,
Touring these memories again.
Devouring my heart with ease,
Let the rainbows face execution.
Let the agony remain deep within me,
now she can soar in deep red skies.
Loved in autumn and drowned in winter.

Burned By Lust

Fusing two hearts by fire,
Her soul was burned by lies.
My heart was torn into bits.
Coming together by moonlight,
Fear the pain of desperation.
our last stand is by the flames.
Burned by lust,
the world fades into glass shards.
Bleeding wounds by tonight,
loved by a grave.
Waiting by an anguished sea,
Touching her paled lips again.
Racing thoughts of painful joy.
Lips as cold as winter,
Heart as warm as a thousand hells.
I love her with all that I can,
No demonic fool can take mine.
As the world sleeps,
we will love like a fallen race.
A thousand nails racing towards me,
my heart will not flinch away from her.
Enter the fumes of romance,
empty hearts run away.
A corrupted smile turned away,
let the roses die by blood.
Come to me my darling,
into the snow like fugitives.

We are not a show for the damned.
Inside a new world,
just the two.
Loving beyond all boundaries
until life blends into Death.

Rising Lust

Moonlight brings romance,
a moment between breaths.
Beautiful as a black-winged angel,
even whales now before her.
Days fade into history as
Demons are burned in Hell's' fire.
Take me away from this tragedy,
climbing madness within my mind.
I can't see the end to my rising lust.
Flying through ghost flames,
just to taste your lips.
My heart pounds like a global war,
basking in her love drives me crazy.
Down into a pool of sweet sweat.
Waiting by thunder's open door.
Come to my silver arms,
her kisses are life itself.
Amid my rising lust,
her touch cools my body.
One kiss burns me like lightning.
Sexy words have made a priest blush,
and let the angels rage in their jealousy.
Her rising lust is a volcano,
inflamed by a deep lengthy romance.

A Hanging Desire

Firelight glows by night,
Two worlds alone in a moment.
Silent is autumn's song,
a hanging desire lost in a tranquil space.
cool breeze swirls by an ancient door,
Sitting by the fire.
Torn like a bad check,
Her eyes were lost in sadness.
A lingering desire is like a vapor,
stale and past its life expectancy.
Shadows flicker between the flames,
silver coffee cup now tarnished from pain.
Her face was pale like white velvet,
No words were spoken.
The night is peaceful,
empty thoughts drown in my mind.
Torn like curtains,
trapped by tempered anguish.
No tears, not even for my dark sins.
Like a ship hidden by fog,
her life was without a lighthouse.
Misdirected by false truths.
Now dead at the table,
Glow of candles continues to dance.
Now a door closes as I walk out.

Ghost Heart

Touched by a fainting romance,
Standing on the last lonely bridge.
Angry with this fickle breeze,
a ghost heart sings by sunset.
Wishing for an end to humanity's darkness,
yet bound by a holy oath to love.
A bitter sorrow rests on my spirit.
A ghost heart beats in a sour fog,
somewhere over the waters,
a haunting sound comes.
A voice from a black despairing darkness,
full of energy.
Splintering the thorns of immorality.
Radiate in passion,
her smile can turn my blood blue.
Roses bow in awe.
Haunting with delight.
Standing in a sea of corpses,
only the moon can relate.
A tale of soft remorse.
Bemoan a wicked fate,
a lover burned at sunrise.
Yet in a bitter fear,
this old moon vacated her spear.
A chance to save,
now broken in disgrace.
Backed away from our graves,

never to see the sun wave.
A ghost heart remains,
to weep another thousand years.

Ghostly Desire

Trapped by death,
sentenced to hell.
Only wanted a faithful wife,
but was rewarded a demoness.
Died by my iron hands,
and so did he.
Blood can't be washed away,
never asked why.
Now I can die.
Her ghostly smile never lied,
a new love from beyond.
Cold is my hands,
as a creepy song plays.
Night falls over the world above,
Trapped by a casket above me.
Pain tickling at my flesh,
reliving every moment in my grave.
A knock perhaps or wishful thinking.
A silent voice calls out,
echoing in my death chamber.
A moment of endless pain,
a deep longing for her sweet arms.
Yet turned away from love,
not by the Spirit but by the evil in her heart.
Now time is dripping away,
waiting for the gates of hell to open.
Ancient justice is always there,

for evil people like me.
Into the despairing darkness,
Chains surround my soul.
Pulling me into my new prison,
no relief from my sentence.
Taunted by her screams of hellish agony.

Thunder's Kiss

Beautiful as night,
silent like death.
Once alone in an empty building,
wasting away like rotting food.
She arrived like Christmas morning,
Touching my frail life with kindness.
Eyes of lavender and tall like an angel.
An empty coffee shop,
two cups steaming with need.
Shy by gentle light,
strong by nature.
A fire burns silently,
her eyes search the endless depths.
for the end of heartache,
slow drips of blood fall in anguish.
Like a wino trying to get the last drop.
A curtain of life and death,
weary and broken like a china plate.
Hidden behind a thousand-year-old guardian,
her heart still melts like butter.
A smile waits in these blazing shadows.
By a fallen oak tree,
I watch with despair.
Knowing it would be easier for
me to get a kiss by thunder than for me
to capture her heart.

As She Cries

As she cries,
my mind trembles from anger.
A deceptive wench this world became,
always consuming more and more.
My lover is dying,
Inside a demon pounds against this shell.
As I shake from a violent rage,
darkness surrounds me like a cloak.
As she cries,
dark hate flows from me.
even the night becomes fearful.
torn heart by a city that breeds iniquity.
Her cold breath makes me want to wage war.
Her eyes remain sad,
even when we walk under a red moon.
Alone except for the hate in this city.
Flames of a white rose,
grey on an old lady.
Our hearts can fly by light.
Touched by desire under distress,
I ache to taste her again.
A single moment of love
can destroy hell.
In a single kiss,
I can bring life to the dead.
She will no longer need to cry.

Love can weep

Lonely is a heart,
broken like a toaster.
Tossed into a trash bin
full of rotting cadavers.
Love can weep on the gallows.
A frosty rusty blade in my heart,
Her words are my grave.
A passionate kiss drives me insane,
Touching my neck with eagerness.
Covered in dark red blood,
droplets glisten like rubies.
Love can weep like a lost virgin.
Love can weep over a
dying rainbow.
Let me touch your wounds
with silver dreams and golden tears.
Time tries to free the light,
rigid resistance denies love.
A kiss to change destiny,
Lost in her sea of tenderness.

Dragon Twilight

smile driving evil away,
Lushes eyebrows wave gently.
Night sits in a coffee shop,
whispering sweet love notes.
Down a street of bones,
across the avenue of sorrow.
A cafe of romance remains,
Lonely ghouls remain outside.
Rise my dragon queen,
consume the liars, unfaithful, thieves,
and murderers, and last with fire from hell.
Open up their hearts before they die,
As rain falls on both the good and wicked,
Heaven's grace is like food; available for all.
Come my dragon queen,
let your wings unfurl.
take my rusted heart into
your mouth.
Let these beautiful flames renew my love,
even as shadows groan under Death's weight.
My struggle becomes a mountain of gold.
Take away these scars of suicide tonight.
Let me drown in your sexy wine.
Be my dragon forever, even until
the fall of heaven.

Lovers Inferno

Two pm, a fire rages.
Two lonely people collide together,
colliding like angels and demons.
A swirling cloud of passion surrounds
the city of death.
Dark frowns in cold alleys,
plotting murder and assault of the body.
Even as evil plots,
light protects love.
Consuming all in an inferno of flame
and pain.
Intertwined roses by time,
Her lips are as soft as goose feathers.
Not one stroke of a katana can sever
our bond.
Can succubus's dream of love?
Even days must end for new ones,
Bound by true cravings for her alone.
A cold cup of coffee cannot warm itself,
action must be applied at the right time.
Yet lost in my mind,
some sanity remains as I contemplate.
Send in a thousand violets,
the evening is cold like my dinner.
My soul shivers at her presence.
This mere hour felt like a bad carnival ride.
In tune with love,

holding her gently is my bliss.
More like a naughty treat before bedtime.
Her fire never grows cold,
A cruel design of a greedy world.
She can't always be so kind.
Let romance grow,
let it age in this rotting world.

As the Wind Blows

As the wind blows,
ten angels will cry.
Your love is rich,
full of pain and sorrow.
Dressed in paled black,
eyes faded by fake romance.
Scalpel to the heart
evil smiles long past.
As the wind blows,
five demons will die.
You stand in a depressed rain,
Waiting in a four-foot pool of blood.
Shadows fall into despair,
yet a wild river remains within you.
As the wind blows,
Your icy smile will be warm again.
Sunlight will bring joy to spring.
All of the colorless tears will
dry up like the Mojave Desert.
Angels will have glorious dreams,
Hell will have its full of empty people.
Love can weep without fear,
Orange roses will bow to the queen.
We can grow old like unicorns,
and die under a cold moonlight.

Nitro Love

Shackles bind me,
paraded by a thousand dead.
Scorned by an archangel,
undressed by a goat.
Tossed into a creepy cell,
yet the flames of love remain.

As a shade whispers,
Gaap hides in a cold guard room.
Years pass without remorse,
silent lips tell no tales.
three hundred jail mates,
Three hundred executions.
A scarlet rose blooms quietly,
covered by shadows of past lives.

Frigid kiss, hot heart

a gentle voice,
eyes as gorgeous as an angry sea.
grey walls fading into oblivion,
her petals spread wide and upwards.
Unbelievable glory unfolds,
turned toward me with haste.
Erase my prison,
Erase all misery.
Touch my tired eyes,
charm me with golden truth.
Exiled from society,
her desire is to be wanted.
Life stolen from ancient youth
lost among fallen stars.
Only to grow as a rose,
inside a forgotten cell.
Cherish this hour,
her tears are my sins.
Inside the pain,
my soul was rotting.
Till the cage was unlocked,
sorrow swept through like
a blade, and not one was alive.

Black Rose

Even as darkness remains frigid,
she will be beautiful like a black rose.
A midnight kiss by rustling chains is arising,
just like fresh blood stains on a surgical table.
May a thousand false gods burn in hell for her pleasure.
Slow drips of wine on my neck,
a fantastic horrid scream from a dying devil girl.
My love turns all wicked spirits into pure love flames.
Her smile charms all silly evil doers,
yet ignores their ignorant pleas for freedom.
tick tock of a fallen crimson clock,
flowers spread their wings.
A fallen sun weeps before her,
the black rose only calls to the pure.
Wicked hearts will roast over black flames.
Her words are hurricanes in a selfish world,
Time is cloaked by a thousand angry angels.
Under a dark sky,
Her lips teases mine.
No more dreams of the dead,
Loneliness is a razor blade to my throat.
Sunlight of tomorrow may never come,
by a crows hunger, ghouls will die.
This is the hour,
In the fog of death, she will come.

When Darkness Loves

Vanished dreams falling
Like rain.
Ruby light drips away tonight,
a shadow stands far away.
Underneath a lonely oak,
Watching silver stars sparkle.
Bound by ancient laws,
Anxiety drips like honey.
Grown accustomed to silence,
her heart is weak as an alcoholic to their next taste.
When darkness loves,
This world burns away.
Shadows melt as wax on candles,
Demons dream of salvation and peace.
Roses never die,
the sapphire sky never lies.
Cold are the lips of romance,
Yet she yearns for her hero.
Turning away from silence and decay,
Her heart burns within.
Take away all pain,
Send it back to hell.
When darkness loves,
Her smile is sweet like
Fresh blood on a cornerstone.

No. 6

Rigid chains on wrists,
Rusty smile faded by
a dark fire.
Lustful words become a prison cell,
Green eyes flicker in the night.
Wild wolves howl,
Naked sprites glide by.
Amber sun glows softly,
Her breath is like wine,
Intoxicating and alluring
like a nude fallen angel.
She is my fallen angel,
Black wings are eight feet in width.
Rusted chains groan,
By an hour's end,
She comes to me.
A broken human death
and disease,
Demanding to devour my
Demons.
Take the storm of love at
full might into our midst.
Never take away my number six,
Don't let these ghouls rip her apart.
Lift my chains to the dark suns,
let my love turn into war
and may they roast in hell forever.

Thousand Shades of Black

Turn back the sands of time,
Alone on a dune of bitter regret.
Stones run into despair,
A heart that beats sadly.
Words lost in dying ink, the
Like a sinking Titanic.
Life is no friend to the lonely.
Tourniquet for the dead,
Devils deal with the corrupted.
Black stars won't lie,
a new love blossoms tonight.
A thousand shades of black,
a lifetime ruined by selfish girls.
Now vengeance is heavens.
Blind thoughts, valueless words
in a loveless world.
As a fire dies,
romance blooms once more.
Eyes of a greenish passion,
alone by the lake of sorrow.
Beaten down by a raging infant,
her soft voice echoes across
the city of the dead.
In blinding darkness,
my heart hears her.
A trickle of blood
and broken bones.

I'll crawl through the dung
of this world for her.
Untouched by filthy hands
Of humanity.
Her soul can not be bought by
the stupidity of human intelligence.
Dressed by divine wisdom,
loved and adored by elite angels.
A swarming desire is for the faithfulness
of love and her only soulmate.
Never tempting the rotting fruits of dating.
Ever annoyed by pathetic pickup lines,
Disgusted at the darkness of all shallow
hearts.
She remains a thousand shades of black
until my death.

My Poison

Amid the fire,
I'll drink my poison.
Shadows of hate ride from empty streets,
Her heart is a castle.
Her love poisons my body,
No one else is true.
True like Death's aim,
into the shallows of hell.
I will go to love her.
As arrows devour my flesh,
and demons drink of my life.
My sapphire heart cannot deny,
My dedication to her.
A thousand demons
may wage war against me.
I am devoted to my poison eternity.
Humanity may dance among the graves,
My soul yearns for her gentle touch.
Hold me until the seven devils are dead,
our lips shall never taste death.
Naked under a fiery blue twilight,
Touched by a golden angel wing.
Bliss sweeping in like a wave,
Tasted heaven once more.

Black Sunset

Daybreak blushes,
Lips stained by blood.
Corrupted by desire,
Breaking away from a damned world.
Standing in the rain
of fallen idol,
Hands woven together,
rebelling against time.
Black Sunset hides our animalistic needs,
Her pale blue eyes feast
on my heart.
Her breasts are heaven's gate.
Slow drips of blue blood cover them.
As winter spreads over us,
fragile beats of a Lost heart are growing.
Touched by pains of yesteryear, torn like a dress.
I remain lost without a moment of light.
Hands collect my spirit,
a glowing smile warms my icy mind.
Now I can die by the knife of love.

Ruby Moonlight

Fiery eyes set my soul in fire,
demanding my full attention.
No time for distractions,
Only pain from whips and chains.
Darken room infused with perfume of hell and fervor.
Blindfolded and bound to
Pleasure, faithful lover that destroyed my heart.
Only her kiss brings me to life,
lightening is jealous and so are adulterous people.
Taken by the demons wrath,
her love kills darkness with ease.
A razor blade weeps bloody tears,
a sweaty aroma sticks to my chest.
Dark light burns angerly,
Taking my body to a new level.
Hands tease in the cold dark, lips taste my riches.
A hundred stars turn away and blush.
Taking her sorrows and making them my scars.
Little demons cradle the grave in fear,
our passion is like a thousand earthquakes.
We can die under a ruby moonlight.
We can die under a ruby moonlight.

Michael Dimenco

Also by Michael Dimenco

Dark Romance
When Darkness Loves

Also by Wolffe

Dark Romance
When Darkness Loves